Fun for Kids & Parents

Playmore Inc., Publishers
and
Waldman Publishing Corporation
New York, NY

*All the recipes in this book must be done with parental
or other adult participation and supervision.
These recipes are not meant for children to do on their own.*

Cover photo courtesy of Lillian Vernon.
www.lillianvernon.com or 1-800-LILLIAN

We wish to thank the following for contributing their recipes:

American Dairy Association
www.ilovecheese.com

BUSH's Baked Beans
www.bushbeans.com

California Raisin Marketing Board
www.calraisins.org

Chicken of the Sea International
www.chickenofthesea.com

Dole® Food Company, Inc.
www.dole5aday.com or 1-800-232-8888

Gold Medal®
www.BettyCrocker.com or 1-800-328-1144

Home Baking Association
www.homebaking.org

Kraft Foods Inc.
www.kraftfoods.com

Land O'Lakes®, Inc.
www.landolakes.com

National Peanut Board
www.nationalpeanutboard.org

National Pork Board
www.otherwhitemeat.com

Popcorn Board
www.popcorn.org

Produce for Better Health Foundation®
www.5aday.com

Texas Beef Council
www.txbeef.org

USA Rice Federation
www.ricecafe.com

Wheat Foods Council
www.wheatfoods.org

Funny Face Grilled Cheese

Ingredients

8 slices LAND O LAKES® Pasteurized Process Cheese Food Singles

8 slices sandwich bread

3 tablespoons LAND O LAKES® Butter, softened

Steps

1. Heat griddle or frying pan.
2. To assemble each sandwich, place 2 slices of cheese on 1 slice of bread.
3. From remaining bread slices, cut out eyes, nose and mouth using small cookie cutters or a knife to make faces.
4. Place cut-out bread slices over cheese to form sandwiches.
5. Spread outside of sandwiches with butter.
6. Place sandwiches, cut-out side down, on griddle.
7. Cook over medium heat until golden brown (2 to 4 minutes).
8. Turn; cook until golden brown (1 to 2 minutes).

Beef and Cheese Pinwheels

Ingredients
12 oz. thinly sliced deli roast beef
1 package (8 oz.) herb-flavored cream cheese
4 large flour tortillas (about 10")
2 cups spinach leaves (about 20 leaves)
1 jar (7 oz.) roasted red peppers, rinsed and drained

Steps
1. Spread cheese evenly over one side of each tortilla.
2. Place deli roast beef over cheese, leaving 1/2" border around edges.
3. Place spinach leaves over beef.
4. Arrange peppers down center over spinach.
5. Roll up tightly and wrap in plastic wrap.
6. Refrigerate at least 30 minutes or up to 6 hours before serving.
7. To serve, cut each roll crosswise into 8 slices.
Arrange cut side up on serving platter.

Banana Peanut Butter Sandwich

Ingredients

2 tablespoons peanut butter

4 slices raisin bread

1 firm, small Dole® banana, peeled and sliced

Steps

1. Spread peanut butter on 2 bread slices.
2. Arrange banana slices over peanut butter.
3. Top with remaining bread.
4. Place sandwiches on cutting board and cut into quarters.

PITA POCKETS WITH CHINESE CHICKEN-PEANUT SALAD

Ingredients

2 cups chopped cooked chicken

1 cup grated carrots

1/2 head roughly chopped iceberg lettuce (about 4 cups)

2/3 cup chow mein noodles

1/3 cup canned sliced water chestnuts

4 tablespoons peanut oil

3 tablespoons creamy peanut butter

3 tablespoons seasoned rice vinegar

1 tablespoon lite soy sauce

1 tablespoon sugar

1/4 cup chopped dry roasted peanuts

2 tablespoons chopped green onions

3 pita breads, cut in half

Steps

1. In a large bowl, mix together chicken, carrots, lettuce, chow mein noodles and water chestnuts. Set aside.
2. To make dressing: In a separate bowl, mix together peanut oil, peanut butter, rice vinegar, soy sauce and sugar until smooth.
3. Stir in peanuts and green onions. Stir until well blended.
4. Pour dressing over salad and toss well.
5. Fill 6 pita pocket halves with even portions of chicken salad.

Deviled Eggs in a Bag

Ingredients

6 hard-cooked eggs

2 tablespoons mayonnaise, sour cream or plain yogurt

3/4 teaspoon prepared mustard

1/2 teaspoon lemon juice, herb or seasoning blend

1/4 teaspoon salt, optional

1/8 teaspoon pepper

Steps

1. Cut eggs in half lengthwise.
2. Set whites aside.
3. Place yolks in 1-quart food storage bag.
4. Add remaining ingredients. Press out air.
5. Seal bag. Knead until yolk mixture is well blended.
6. Push yolk mixture toward corner. Snip about 1/2 inch off corner.
7. Squeezing bag gently, fill reserved whites with yolk mixture.
   Chill to blend flavors.

TUNA TRIANGLES

INGREDIENTS

1 CAN (12 OZ.) CHICKEN OF THE SEA® SOLID WHITE OR CHUNK LIGHT TUNA,
   WELL DRAINED AND FLAKED
1 CUP SHREDDED CHEDDAR CHEESE
2 TABLESPOONS RANCH-STYLE DRESSING
1 CAN (8 OZ.) REFRIGERATED CRESCENT
   ROLL DOUGH
CHOPPED PEPPERS, ONION,
   CELERY OR OLIVES (OPTIONAL)

STEPS

1. COMBINE TUNA, CHEESE AND DRESSING. IF DESIRED, UP TO 1/4 CUP CHOPPED
   PEPPERS, ONION, CELERY OR OLIVES MAY BE ADDED TO THE MIXTURE.
2. SEPARATE CRESCENT DOUGH INTO FOUR RECTANGLES. ON AN UNGREASED
   BAKING SHEET, PRESS EACH RECTANGLE TO ABOUT 4"x8".
   CUT EACH RECTANGLE IN HALF TO FORM EIGHT SQUARES.
3. MOUND TUNA MIXTURE ON A DIAGONAL HALF OF EACH SQUARE, LEAVING A 1/2"
   BORDER AROUND THE FILLING. FOLD DOUGH SQUARES IN HALF TO FORM TRIANGLES;
   PRESS EDGES WITH FORK TO SEAL, AND CUT A SLIT IN TOP.
4. BAKE AT 375° FOR 14 TO 16 MINUTES UNTIL GOLDEN BROWN.

SUGAR CORN SNACK ATTACK

Ingredients

1/2 cup unpopped popcorn
3 tablespoons white sugar
1/4 cup vegetable oil
    for popping

Steps

1. Heat oil in medium-sized pan until hot.
2. Add popcorn and sprinkle all of the sugar over it.
3. Cover and shake continuously until popped.

"Monkey See, Monkey Dough"

Ingredients

2 cups Gold Medal® all-purpose flour
1 tablespoon sugar
3 teaspoons baking powder
1 teaspoon salt
1/2 cup shortening
3/4 cup milk
1/3 cup grated Parmesan cheese
1 teaspoon Italian seasoning
2 tablespoons butter or margarine, melted

Steps

1. Heat oven to 425°.
2. Stir flour, sugar, baking powder and salt in medium bowl until mixed.
3. Cut shortening into flour mixture, by crisscrossing with 2 knives, until crumbly.
4. Stir in milk until a soft dough forms.
5. Put dough on lightly floured surface, and shape into a ball, using floured hands. Knead dough by folding and pushing with the palms of your hands, then make a quarter turn. Repeat these steps to knead 10 times. Divide dough into 32 pieces.
6. Mix cheese and Italian seasoning.
7. Roll dough pieces in cheese mixture. Some mixture will be left.
8. Put pieces in ungreased round pan, 9"x1-1/2".
9. Sprinkle with rest of cheese mixture. Drizzle butter over the top.
10. Bake 15 to 20 minutes or until light golden brown. Take bread out of pan, and serve warm.
11. For dipping, serve with tomato sauce, cheese sauce or pizza sauce that you have heated, if you like.

JAMMIN' TUNA Q

Ingredients

1 can (12 oz.) Chicken of the Sea® Light Chunk Tuna, drained
12 oz. barbecue sauce
4 poppy seed Kaiser rolls
4 lettuce leaves
3 slices of tomato
Chopped red onion and chopped sweet pepper (optional garnish)

Steps

1. Heat tuna and barbecue sauce over medium heat for 5 minutes.
2. Split buns and toast; top with lettuce and tomato slices.
3. Spoon tuna mixture on top and sprinkle with onion and pepper; cover with bun.

TEX MEX MIX

Ingredients

2 quarts popcorn popped in oil
2 teaspoons ground chili powder
2 teaspoons paprika
2 teaspoons ground cumin
1 cup cubed Monterey Jack cheese (abut 1/4" cubes)

Steps

1. Keep popped popcorn warm.
2. Mix seasonings together and toss with popcorn.
3. Add cheese and mix thoroughly.

BLT TUNA BURGER

Ingredients

1 can (12 oz.) Chicken of the Sea® Solid White Tuna in water
1/2 cup breadcrumbs, unseasoned
3 tablespoons cooked and crumbled bacon bits
1/2 cup light mayonnaise
4 burger buns (2 oz.)
4 lettuce leaves
8 tomato slices

Steps

1. Drain tuna. Flake tuna in large mixing bowl.
2. Add breadcrumbs and bacon bits to tuna and combine.
3. Mix in mayonnaise until all ingredients are well combined.
4. Refrigerate mixture until ready to form into burgers.
5. Form into 4 burgers and place on waxed paper.
6. Open buns and place lettuce leaves on bun halves.
7. Cook burgers in non-stick pan or griddle just until lightly browned and hot throughout, turning once.
8. Place burgers on lettuce; top with tomato slices (2 per burger) and bun top.
9. Serve immediately.

Monkey Face Sandwich

Ingredients
16 slices whole wheat bread
1 package (6 oz.) OSCAR MAYER® Boiled Ham
8 KRAFT® Singles
MIRACLE WHIP® Salad Dressing
Raisins

Steps
1. Place bread slices on cutting board. Cut into 3" circles using cookie cutter or sharp knife.
2. Repeat with ham and Singles. Reserve scraps.
3. Spread 8 of the bread circles with salad dressing.
4. Top each with ham, Singles and second bread circle.
5. Decorate with additional salad dressing and raisins to make monkey faces.
6. Use reserved scraps to make monkey ears.

Pup-Tent Pie

Ingredients

1/2 pound hot dogs, sliced
1 can (15 oz.) pork and beans
1 can (8 oz.) tomato sauce
3 tablespoons packed brown sugar
1-1/2 cups Gold Medal® all-purpose flour
2 teaspoons baking powder
1/2 teaspoon salt
2/3 cup water
3 tablespoons butter or margarine, melted

Steps

1. Heat oven to 450°.
2. Stir hot dogs, pork and beans, tomato sauce and brown sugar in ungreased 9" square pan until mixed.
3. Bake about 15 minutes or until bubbly.
4. Stir other ingredients in medium bowl until a soft dough forms.
5. Drop dough by 8 spoonfuls onto hot dog mixture.
6. Bake 15 to 20 minutes or until dumplings are golden brown.

BALLPARK POPCORN CRUNCH

Ingredients

1/2 cup butter
1/2 cup brown sugar
3 quarts unsalted popped popcorn
1 cup chopped walnuts

Steps

1. Cream together butter and brown sugar till light and fluffy.
2. In a separate bowl, toss popcorn and walnuts. Add creamed mixture to popcorn and nuts. Combine until coated.
3. Spread on a large baking sheet in a single layer.
4. Bake at 350° for 10 minutes or until crisp.

Paddle Cookie Pops

Ingredients

1 cup sugar
1 cup butter or margarine, softened
1/2 teaspoon vanilla
1 egg
2-2/3 cups Gold Medal® all-purpose flour
3 food colors (your favorite colors)
About 48 flat wooden sticks with rounded ends

Steps

1. Heat oven to 375°.
2. Stir sugar, butter, vanilla and egg in large bowl until smooth. Stir in flour.
3. Divide dough into 3 equal parts.
4. Stir 4 drops of 1 food color into each part of dough to make 3 different colors of dough.
5. Shape dough into 1" balls, using a bit of each color of dough for each ball.
6. Put balls 2" apart on ungreased cookie sheet.
7. Poke a wooden stick into side of each ball.
8. Press balls until 1/4" thick, using the bottom of a glass dipped in sugar.
9. Bake 9 to 11 minutes or until slightly firm and edges are light golden brown.
10. Cool 1 minute before taking cookies off cookie sheet. Cool completely. Frost and decorate cookies, if you like.

Eggs Jose

Ingredients

Butter
1 egg
1 tablespoon shredded
  Monterey Jack cheese
1 teaspoon water
1 tablespoon salsa or taco sauce
1 small tortilla

Steps

1. Heat enough butter over medium heat to grease a small skillet until hot enough to sizzle a drop of water.
2. Break and slip egg into skillet.
3. Top with cheese.
4. Add water.
5. Cover skillet tightly to hold in steam. Reduce heat to low.
6. Cook until white is completely set and yolk thickens but is not hard.
7. Spread salsa on tortilla. Top with egg.

Alphabet Sandwiches

Ingredients

4 slices of your favorite sliced bread
4 to 8 slices of part-skim mozzarella or American cheese
(depends on size of cookie cutters)
Alphabet or other cookie cutters
Vegetables, pepperoni, olives (optional)

Steps

1. Cut each slice of bread into two letters – perhaps spelling your initials; place on a baking sheet.
(Save leftover bread for stuffing or bread pudding).
2. Cut cheese with the same cookie cutter and place directly on top of the bread. Decorate with pieces of vegetables, pepperoni or olives.
3. Bake for 3 to 4 minutes just until the cheese is soft but does not run down the sides. Cool slightly before serving.

Grilled Cheese and Pickle Sandwich

Ingredients
4 slices yellow American cheese
4 slices Muenster cheese, thinly sliced
Dill pickles, sliced lengthwise
8 slices sourdough bread

Steps
1. Heat a large, heavy skillet or griddle over medium heat (about 300°).
2. Place one slice of American cheese on sourdough bread, top with 4 dill pickle slices, slice of Muenster cheese and second slice of bread. Continue with remaining ingredients to make four sandwiches.
3. Lightly butter one side of each sandwich (or coat with butter-flavored cooking spray) and place buttered side down on skillet griddle.
4. Butter the top slice of each sandwich.
5. Grill slowly on both sides until cheese has melted and bread has browned. Serve warm.

POPCORN CHIPWICHES

Ingredients

2-1/2 quarts popped popcorn
1-1/2 cups light brown sugar
3/4 cup dark corn syrup
1/2 cup butter
1 tablespoon vinegar
1/2 teaspoon salt
1 package (6 oz.) chocolate pieces
1/2 cup chopped walnuts
2 pints brick-style vanilla ice cream

Steps

1. Keep popcorn warm.
2. In a three-quart saucepan, combine brown sugar, corn syrup, butter, vinegar and salt.
3. Cook and stir until sugar dissolves. Continue to cook until hard ball stage (250° on a candy thermometer).
4. Pour syrup over popped popcorn; stir to coat.
5. Add chocolate pieces and nuts; stir just to mix.
6. Pour into two 13"x9"x2" pans, spreading and packing firmly. Cool.
7. In each pan, cut 12 rectangles.
8. Cut each pint of ice cream into 6 slices. Sandwich ice cream between two popcorn rectangles.

Katy's Best Egg Salad

Ingredients

1/4 cup mayonnaise

1 tablespoon sweet pickle relish

1/2 teaspoon prepared mustard

1/4 teaspoon salt

4 hard cooked eggs

1/2 stalk celery, washed and
chopped into dime-size pieces

Steps

1. Put the mayonnaise, relish, mustard and salt into a medium bowl.
2. Stir well.
3. Chop the eggs with a knife or an egg slicer.
4. Stir the eggs and celery into the mayonnaise mixture.

Barbecued Chicken Toasties

Ingredients

can (5 to 6.75 oz.) chunk
or shredded chicken, drained
tablespoon bottled barbecue sauce
slices whole-wheat sandwich bread
eggs
tablespoons milk
Carrot slices, optional

Steps

. In a small bowl, stir the chicken and barbecue sauce.
. Spread about 2 tablespoons of chicken mixture on 3 slices of bread.
. Top the mixture with the rest of the slices to make sandwiches.
. Beat the eggs and milk until they are well blended.
. Pour mixture into a shallow dish, pie pan or cake pan.
. Carefully place one of the chicken sandwiches in the egg mixture.
. Let it stand 2 or 3 minutes.
. Carefully turn over with a pancake turner. Let stand for another 2 to 3 minutes.
. Put on a greased cookie sheet. Repeat with the other sandwiches.
0. Bake all the sandwiches on the cookie sheet in preheated 400º
   oven for 8 minutes on each side.
1. Cut each sandwich into 4 pieces. Stand the pieces up on a plate.
2. Use carrot slices to make wheels for your toasties, if you like.

Italian Pork Hoagie

Ingredients

6 boneless pork loin chops, cut into thin strips
1/3 cup reduced-fat Italian dressing
1/3 cup pizza sauce
6 thin slices mozzarella cheese
6 hot dog buns

Steps

1. In a heavy plastic bag, combine pork strips and dressing;
refrigerate several hours or overnight.
2. Drain off marinade, discarding excess.
3. Heat a 12" non-stick skillet over medium-high heat;
add pork strips to the pan and cook, stirring frequently
for 8 minutes or until pork strips are lightly browned.
4. Divide pork strips into 6 equal portions and place on bottom halves of buns.
5. Spoon on 1 tablespoon of pizza sauce for each sandwich.
6. Top with slice of mozzarella cheese.
7. Bake in a 350° oven for 5 minutes,
or until cheese melts and bun is lightly toasted.

TASTES-LiKE-A-HOT-DOG-SPECIAL

Ingredients
Ketchup
1 hot dog bun
Mustard
1 scrambled egg
Sweet pickle relish

Steps
1. Spread ketchup on one side of a hot dog bun and mustard on the other.
2. Spoon the egg onto the bun.
3. Top with a spoonful of sweet pickle relish.

Raisin Cereal Pops

Ingredients

5 cups crisp rice cereal
3 cups California raisins
1/4 cup margarine
1 package (10 oz.) marshmallows
1/3 cup presweetened fruit flavor
   powdered drink mix
12 (7 oz.) paper cups
12 wooden sticks
   (available at hobby and craft stores), if desired

Steps

1. In large bowl, combine cereal and raisins. Set aside.
2. In medium saucepan, melt margarine. Add marshmallows. Cook and stir over very low heat until marshmallows are melted and mixture is smooth.
3. Stir in drink mix powder. Pour over cereal and raisin mixture; mix well.
4. Lightly spray fingers and paper cups with non-stick cooking spray.
5. Firmly pack mixture into sprayed cups. If using wooden sticks, push one all the way to the bottom of each cup.
6. Cool completely. When ready to serve, turn cups upside down and tap bottoms to remove pops.

Sweet and Crunchy Munch Mix

Ingredients

3 cups POST® Frosted Shredded Wheat Cereal
2 cups caramel popcorn
2 cups small pretzels
1 cup candy-coated milk chocolate candies

Steps

1. Mix all ingredients in large bowl.
2. Store in tightly covered container.

Cool Grapes

Ingredients
1 large bunch of seedless green or red grapes

Steps
1. Wash the grapes and remove the stems.
2. Arrange grapes on a baking sheet and place in the freezer for 30 minutes.
3. Remove from freezer and enjoy.
4. Store remaining frozen grapes in plastic bags in the freezer.

PARMESAN POPCORN

Ingredients
2 quarts (8 cups) popped popcorn
1/4 cup (1/2 stick) butter or margarine, melted
1/4 cup KRAFT® 100% Grated Parmesan Cheese
Salt (optional)

Steps
1. Toss popcorn with butter and cheese.
2. Season to taste with salt.
3. Sprinkle with additional cheese, if desired.

BAGEL TUNA MELT

Ingredients

3 to 4 bagels, sliced into halves

1 can (12 oz.) Chicken of the Sea® Solid White Albacore or Chunk Light Tuna, drained and flaked

1-1/2 cups shredded, reduced-fat Cheddar cheese, divided

1 cup diced apple

2 tablespoons sliced green onions

Steps

1. Place bagels, cut side up, on foil-lined baking sheet.

2. Combine tuna, 1 cup cheese, apple and onion. Spread over sliced bagels. Sprinkle with remaining cheese.

3. Bake at 400° for 6 to 8 minutes or until cheese is melted.

Pumpkin Butter

Ingredients

4 cups canned or fresh pumpkin, pureed
1/2 cup honey
1 tablespoon cinnamon, ground
1/4 teaspoon ginger, ground
1/4 teaspoon cloves, ground
2 tablespoons lemon juice

Steps

1. Combine all ingredients in a large saucepan.
2. Cook on low for 45 minutes, stirring frequently.
3. Pour into jars and cover tightly. Let cool and refrigerate.

Bean Burger

Ingredients

4 frozen, fully-cooked burgers
1/2 cup refried beans
1/4 cup salsa picante
1 bag (1-1/4 oz.) corn chips
  (1/2 cup crushed)
4 hamburger buns
Mayonnaise
Tomato slices
Lettuce leaves

Steps

1. Blend refried beans and salsa in a small bowl.
2. Spread evenly over frozen burgers and place in a microwave-safe dish.
3. Cover with plastic wrap, folding back one corner.
4. Microwave burgers on High 4 to 5 minutes, turning dish halfway through heating time, until burgers are piping hot.
5. Coarsely crush corn chips.
6. Spread mayonnaise on buns. Place lettuce and tomato slices on bottom half of each bun. Top with burgers, bean side up.
7. Sprinkle corn chips evenly over beans. Place remaining buns on top and press gently.

ALL~AMERICAN GRILLED CHEESE
from the kitchen of Mr. Food®

Ingredients

4 tablespoons (1/2 stick) butter, softened
8 slices hearty white bread
8 slices (1/4 lb.) American cheese
16 slices crisp, cooked bacon
8 slices (1/4 lb.) Colby cheese

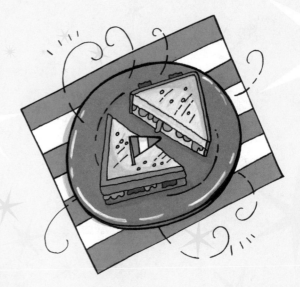

Steps

1. Spread butter evenly on one side of each piece of bread.
2. Distribute American cheese slices and bacon equally over 4 slices of bread on the side without butter.
3. Place Colby cheese slices over the bacon, and top with the remaining slices of bread, butter~side out.
4. Heat a large skillet or griddle over medium heat. Cook sandwiches, in batches if necessary, for 2 to 3 minutes per side, or until golden and the cheeses are melted.
5. Serve immediately.

Bush's® Cheesy Bean Dog Roll-Ups

Ingredients

1 (28 oz.) or 2 (16 oz.) cans of BUSH'S®
  Baked Beans
1 package (16 oz.) of beef franks
8 (8") flour tortillas
6 slices American cheese

Steps

1. Spray 9"x13" baking dish with non-stick coating.
2. Roll hot dog inside a tortilla.
3. Place in baking dish and repeat with remaining hot dogs and tortillas.
4. Top tortilla roll-ups with BUSH'S® Baked Beans and cheese slices.
5. Cover dish with plastic wrap and microwave for 10 minutes,
   turning dish halfway through cooking.

THE ALL-AMERICAN CHEESEBURGER

Ingredients

- √2 cup ketchup
- √4 cup unseasoned bread crumbs
- 1/2 lbs. lean ground beef
- cup crushed potato chips
- cup sweet pickle relish
- slices American cheese, cut into quarters
- 2 mini Kaiser or dinner rolls

Steps

1. Preheat grill.
2. Mix together Ketchup, unseasoned breadcrumbs and ground beef.
3. Form into 12 mini patties for mini cheeseburgers.
4. Grill over medium heat, about 6 to 8 minutes, or until desired doneness.
5. While burgers are cooking, combine crushed potato chips and relish.
6. Top each cooked burger with about 2 tablespoons of potato chip/relish mixture, and then place 2 quarters of the sliced cheese on top.
7. Serve on mini rolls with desired seasonings.

Sunshine Snack Mix

Ingredients
2 cups California raisins
2 cups low-fat granola cereal
1 cup candy-coated chocolate pieces
1/2 cup sunflower nuts

Steps
1. In large bowl, combine all ingredients.
2. Mix well.

Bacon Wrapped Corn Dogs

Ingredients

can (11-1/2 oz.) refrigerated cornbread twists
wooden pop sticks
package (16 oz.) OSCAR MAYER®
Bun-Length Wieners
package (2.1 oz.) OSCAR MAYER®
Ready to Serve Bacon

Steps

1. Separate cornbread dough into 8 sticks, pinching short ends together to seal.
2. Roll or press each piece into 14" rope.
3. Insert wooden sticks lengthwise into wieners, leaving 1" of each stick exposed.
4. Wrap each cornbread rope in spiral fashion around each wiener, pressing ends of dough to seal.
5. Wrap 1 or 2 bacon slices in spiral fashion around each cornbread-covered wiener; press bacon into cornbread.
6. Place on cookie sheet sprayed with no-stick cooking spray.
7. Bake at 350° for 20 minutes or until cornbread is golden brown.
8. Serve with ketchup, KRAFT® Pure Prepared Mustard or honey.

BIG BITES

INGREDIENTS
12 OZ. RED POTATOES, PEELED, COOKED, CUT INTO 1/2" PIECES
2 CUPS (8 OZ.) SHREDDED SWISS CHEESE
1/3 CUP CHOPPED RED PEPPER
1/3 CUP CHOPPED GREEN PEPPER
1 CUP MAYONNAISE OR LIGHT MAYONNAISE
1/2 TEASPOON SALT
1/8 TEASPOON CAYENNE PEPPER
24 SLICES BAKED HAM OR TURKEY
FINELY CHOPPED PARSLEY

STEPS
1. COMBINE POTATOES, SWISS CHEESE, AND RED AND GREEN PEPPERS IN MEDIUM BOWL; STIR IN MAYONNAISE, SALT AND PEPPER.
2. SPOON 2 GENEROUS TABLESPOONS POTATO SALAD ON EACH HAM AND TURKEY SLICE AND ROLL INTO A CORNUCOPIA (OR FUNNEL) SHAPE; SPRINKLE WITH PARSLEY.
3. EAT AT ROOM TEMPERATURE.

QUESO FUNDIDO

Ingredients
2 green onions and tops, sliced
4 large cloves of garlic, minced
2 tablespoons (1/4 stick) butter
6 oz. Pepper-Jack cheese, cut into 1/2" cubes
2 to 4 tablespoons milk
3 oz. chorizo (spicy sausage), casing removed,
   cooked until browned, drained, crumbled
2 tablespoons chopped tomato
2 tablespoons finely chopped cilantro
6 flour tortillas, warm (for wraps)
Chopped or sliced fresh vegetables and
   tortilla chips (optional)

Steps
1. Saute onions and garlic in butter in medium saucepan until tender, 2 to 3 minutes.
2. Add cheese; cook, covered, over medium to medium-low heat until cheese is melted,
   8 to 10 minutes, stirring frequently. Stir in milk if mixture is too thick.
3. Spoon cheese into bowl or small chafing dish; sprinkle with chorizo, tomato, and cilantro.
4. Spoon about 2 tablespoons mixture on each tortilla and roll up for wraps.

Happy Trails Mix

Ingredients

Granola, whole grain cereals, mini pretzels, popcorn, sunflower or pumpkin seeds
Chopped dried fruit: banana chips, apples, cranberries, apricots, raisins,
yogurt covered raisins, dates, pineapple, peaches
Chopped nuts: unsalted peanuts, cashews, walnuts, almonds, macadamia nuts

Steps

1. Make your own special trail mix by mixing desired amounts of the suggestions above or your own favorite ingredients.
2. Mix all ingredients and store in an airtight container.
3. Pack in small plastic bags for easy carrying.

Bruchetta Burger

Ingredients

Cooked hamburger patties
Tomatoes
Fresh basil
Mozzarella
French bread

Steps

1. Start with cooked hamburger patties. (Try one of the burger recipes in this book!)
2. Complement your burger with thickly sliced fresh tomatoes, chopped fresh basil and three slices of mozzarella.
3. Place and serve burgers on toasted garlic french bread.

Cheesy Hot Dog Crescent

Ingredients
8 OSCAR MAYER® Beef Franks
4 KRAFT® Singles, each cut into 4 strips
1 can (8 oz.) refrigerated crescent dinner rolls

Steps
1. Cut a lengthwise pocket into each frank to within 1/2" of ends; insert 2 Singles strips into each pocket.
2. Separate crescent roll dough into triangles; wrap 1 triangle around each frank.
3. Place on ungreased cookie sheet, Singles-side up.
4. Bake at 375° for 12 minutes or until crescent rolls are golden brown.

Cowboy Hamburgers

Ingredients

1 lb. ground beef
2 to 4 cloves garlic, minced
5 to 6 shakes Worcestershire sauce
1/2 teaspoon Cajun seasoning
    (like Tony Chachere's)
1/2 teaspoon salt
1/2 teaspoon pepper
1/4 cup hot or hearty barbecue sauce

Steps

1. In medium bowl, combine all ingredients,
   mixing lightly but thoroughly.
2. Shape into 4 patties.
3. Place patties on grid over medium ash-covered coals.
4. Grill uncovered 14 to 16 minutes or until centers are no longer pink
   and internal thermometer reads 160°, turning once.

Caesar Burger

Ingredients
Cooked hamburger patties
Crusty roll
Caesar dressing
Garlic and black pepper
Romaine lettuce
Avocado slices

Steps
1. Start with cooked hamburger patties.
(Try one of the burger recipes in this book!)
2. Spread a crusty roll with Caesar dressing, season burger with garlic and black pepper, and top with romaine lettuce and avocado slices.

Dino Bone Sub

ngredients

hot dog bun, split
tablespoon MIRACLE WHIP® Salad Dressing
lettuce leaf
slice OSCAR MAYER® Bologna
KRAFT® mozzarella String Cheese

Steps

1. Spread cut sides of bun with salad dressing.
2. Add lettuce.
3. Roll bologna around string cheese.
4. Place in bun.

Happy Trails Rice Mix

Ingredients

2 cups bite-size crispy rice squares
2 cups bite-size crispy corn squares
2 cups puffed rice
1 cup dried banana chips
1 cup dry-roasted peanuts
1 cup chocolate candies
1 cup seedless raisins

Steps

1. In large bowl, combine rice squares, corn squares, puffed rice, banana chips, peanuts, candies and raisins; mix well.
2. Store in tightly covered container.

"Sushi" Snack Bites

Ingredients
2 fruit leather wrappers
1/2 cup semi-sweet white chocolate pieces
1 (10 oz.) bag marshmallows
2 tablespoons milk
3 cups crisp rice cereal
6 worm-shaped gummy candies *
* Dried fruit, licorice, or other candy can
be used as an alternative filling for sushi rolls.

Steps
1. Unwrap fruit leather, remove clear plastic wrap, lay flat on large tray.
2. In large saucepan, combine chocolate pieces, marshmallows and milk.
3. Place saucepan on burner over low heat.
4. Cook, stirring constantly, until chocolate and marshmallows are melted, about 10 minutes.
5. Add cereal to marshmallows; mix well. Turn burner off.
6. Spoon 1/2 cup cereal mixture onto each fruit leather piece.
7. Spread mixture evenly across fruit roll. Press down firmly using back of spoon.
8. Place 3 worm-shaped gummy candies along center of each fruit leather piece.
9. Roll up. Press to seal securely.
10. Cut each roll into 4 pieces.

Fruited Focaccia

INGREDIENTS

1 cup raisins

1/2 cup dried cherries or other dried fruit

1 package (1/4 oz.) fast-rising yeast

1 cup very warm water

2 tablespoons to 1/4 cup sugar or mild honey (to taste)

2-1/2 cups bread flour or all-purpose flour, divided

1/2 cup whole wheat flour

2 tablespoons sunflower or olive oil

1 teaspoon salt

STEPS

1. In a large bowl, stir together the yeast and 1-1/2 cups of the flour.
2. Stir in the water, honey or sugar, oil and salt.
3. Add the whole wheat flour and enough remaining bread flour (about 1-1/2 cups) to make a rough sticky dough ball.
4. Sprinkle the counter with some of the remaining flour. Place the dough on the floured counter, turn it over and knead for about 10 minutes until very smooth.
5. When the dough is kneaded, flatten the dough with your hands. Put the fruit in the middle and overlap the dough over the fruit. Knead and fold carefully to mix in the fruit.
6. Turn the bowl over the dough and let it rest 10 minutes at room temperature.
7. Grease or spray cookie or pizza baking pans. Flatten the dough by hand into a rectangle about 1/2" thick. Place the dough on the pan. Cover with plastic wrap sprayed with pan spray.
8. Let dough rise until doubled in thickness — about 30 to 45 minutes.
9. Dimple the dough by pressing fingertips or thumbs into it, about 1/2" deep and 2" apart, all over the surface of the dough. Cover and let rise again until doubled in thickness.
10. Preheat oven to 400°. While oven is heating, brush top of bread with egg wash.
11. Bake 15 to 20 minutes until golden. Cool on wire racks.
12. Serve warm. Split Fruited Focaccia in half, spread with a favorite dressing and enjoy thin sliced meats, cheeses and sprouts in between.